Transportation

Le transport

leh trons-*paw*

Illustrated by Clare Beaton

Illustré par Clare Beaton

BARRON'S

bicycle

la bicyclette

lah bee-see-*klet*

car

la voiture

lah vwot-*yure*

truck

le camion

leh camee-*oh*

boat

le bateau

leh ba-*toh*

bus

l'autobus

low-toh-boos

fire engine

le camion de pompiers

leh camee-*oh* deh pompee-*eh*

motorcycle

la moto

lah moh-*toh*

tractor

le tracteur

leh tract-*err*

digger

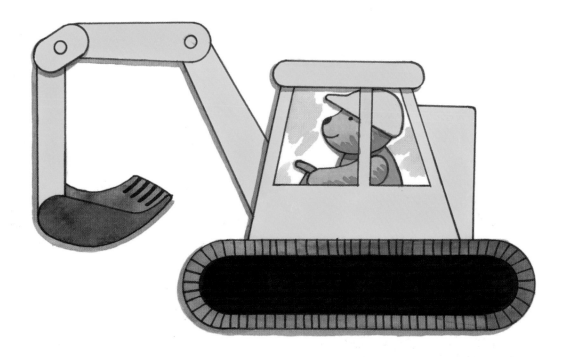

la pelleteuse

lah pellet-*ers*

airplane

l'avion

lavee-oh

train

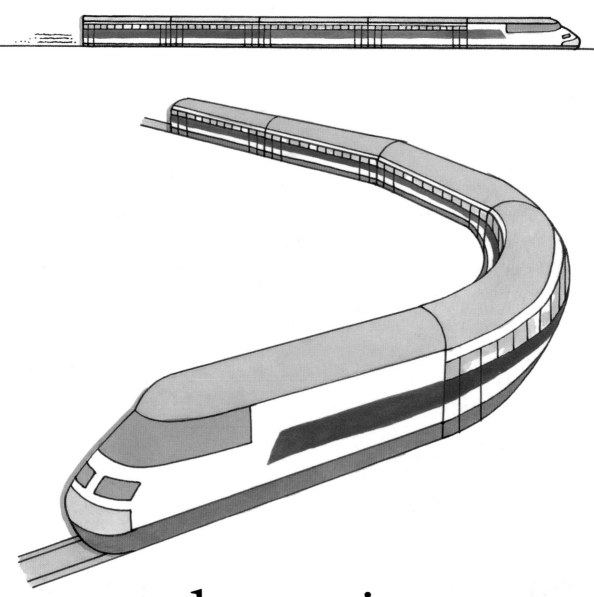

le train

leh trah

A simple guide to pronouncing the French words★

- Read this guide as naturally as possible, as if it were English.
- Put stress on the letters in *italics* e.g. lah vwot-*yure*.
- Remember that the final consonants in French generally are silent.

la bicyclette	lah bee-see-*klet*	**bicycle**
la voiture	lah vwot-*yure*	**car**
le camion	leh camee-*oh*	**truck**
le bateau	leh ba-*toh*	**boat**
l'autobus	low-toh-*boos*	**bus**
le camion de pompiers	leh camee-*oh* deh pompee-*eh*	**fire engine**
la moto	lah moh-*toh*	**motorcycle**
le tracteur	leh tract-*err*	**tractor**
la pelleteuse	lah pellet-*ers*	**digger**
l'avion	lavee-*oh*	**airplane**
le train	leh trah	**train**

★There are many different guides to pronunciation. Our guide attempts to balance precision with simplicity.